TEC

P9-AGS-434

Count On It!

Two

¡Cuenta con ello!

Dos

Dana Meachen Rau

Marshall Cavendish
Benchmark
New York

Two boys.

———◆———

Dos niños.

Two legs.

Dos piernas.

Two eyes.

---❖---

Dos ojos.

Two eggs.

❖

Dos huevos.

Two shoes.

---❖---

Dos zapatos.

11

Two sleds.

---❖---

Dos trineos.

Two wheels.

Dos ruedas.

Two beds.

❖

Dos camas.

Two!

———❖———

¡Dos!

Words We Know
Palabras conocidas

beds
camas

boys
niños

eggs
huevos

eyes
ojos

legs
piernas

shoes
zapatos

sleds
trineos

wheels
ruedas

21

Index

Índice

About the Author

Dana Meachen Rau is the author of many other titles in the Bookworms series, as well as other nonfiction and early reader books. She lives in Burlington, Connecticut, with her husband and two children.

Datos biográficos de la autora

Dana Meachen Rau es la autora de muchos libros de la serie Bookworms y de otros libros de no ficción y de lectura inicial. Vive en Burlington, Connecticut, con su esposo y dos hijos.

With thanks to the Reading Consultants:

Nanci Vargus, Ed.D., is an Assistant Professor of Elementary Education at the University of Indianapolis.

Beth Walker Gambro is an Adjunct Professor at the University of St. Francis in Joliet, Illinois.

Agradecemos a las asesoras de lectura:

Nanci Vargus, Dra. en Ed. y profesora auxiliar de Educación Primaria en la Universidad de Indianápolis.

Beth Walker Gambro, profesora adjunta en la Universidad de St. Francis en Joliet, Illinois.

Marshall Cavendish Benchmark
99 White Plains Road
Tarrytown, New York 10591
www.marshallcavendish.us

Library of Congress Cataloging-in-Publication Data

Rau, Dana Meachen, 1971–
[Dos. Spanish & English]
Two / by Dana Meachen Rau = Dos / por Dana Meachen Rau.
p. cm. – (Bookworms. Count on it! = Bookworms. ¡Cuenta con ello!)
Includes index.
ISBN 978-0-7614-3474-0 (bilingual ed.) – ISBN 978-0-7614-3445-0 (Spanish ed.)
ISBN 978-0-7614-2967-8 (English ed.)
1. Two (The number)–Juvenile literature. 2. Number concept–Juvenile literature.
I. Title. II. Title: Dos. III. Series.
QA141.3.R2818 2009
513–dc22
2008017582

Editor: Christina Gardeski
Publisher: Michelle Bisson
Designer: Virginia Pope
Art Director: Anahid Hamparian

Spanish Translation and Text Composition by Victory Productions, Inc.
www.victoryprd.com

Photo Research by Anne Burns Images

The photographs in this book are used with permission and through the courtesy of:
SuperStock: pp. 1, 11, 21TR BananaStock; pp. 7, 15, 19, 20BR, 21BR age fotostock;
pp. 13, 21BL SuperStock. *Jupiter Images*: pp. 3, 20TR Noble Stock; pp. 5, 21TL Marcie Jan Bronstein;
pp. 9, 20BL Push. *Jay Mallin*: pp. 17, 20TL.

Printed in Malaysia
1 3 5 6 4 2